Introduction

This book introduces some new tools and c
of the previous cutters in the ORCHARD PR
in the other books in this series – Books 1 to
Book 5 'Great Ideas for Cake Decorators' ISE
comprehensive index to all the Books 1 to 5.
References: Throughout this book reference i
intended to mean Triple strength Rose Water ⌐ ᵧ¡ᵤₑ. Egg
white may be used if required. Similarly, 'paste ₌₁₁ₑₐns flowerpaste.

The Tools. General Notes:

Non-stick.   One of their most useful aspects is their non-stick property,
                  which is inherent in the design and material used. It is not a
                  surface finish and, therefore, cannot wear off.

Materials.   All the tools can be used with any soft material such as
                  flowerpaste, sugarpaste, marzipan, modelling chocolate,
                  plasticine, modelling clay etc.

Temperature.   They will withstand boiling water or the dishwasher without
                  deforming.

Handles.   All the cutters have comfortably sized hollow handles which
                  allow you to exert firm pressure over the whole of the
                  cutting edges.

Stability.   They will not rust, corrode, deform or wear out with normal
                  usage.

Marking.   All the tools are permanently marked to aid easy
                  identification.

Metal.   They should not brought into contact with sharp metal
                  objects which may damage the cutting edges or surfaces
                  i.e. keep them separated from metal cutters.

Boards.   Our original non-stick boards (white or green) with their
                  rubber feet and non-stick rolling pins (5" to 23") really do
                  make handling sticky materials more of a pleasure and
                  enable you to roll out your pastes much thinner than you
                  thought possible.

Hygiene.   The materials meet the appropriate EEC regulations for
                  food hygiene.

Endorsement.   All the items are personally endorsed and used by PAT
                  ASHBY, our Technical Director, who is one of the leading
                  teachers of sugarcraft in the UK and is an International
                  Judge.

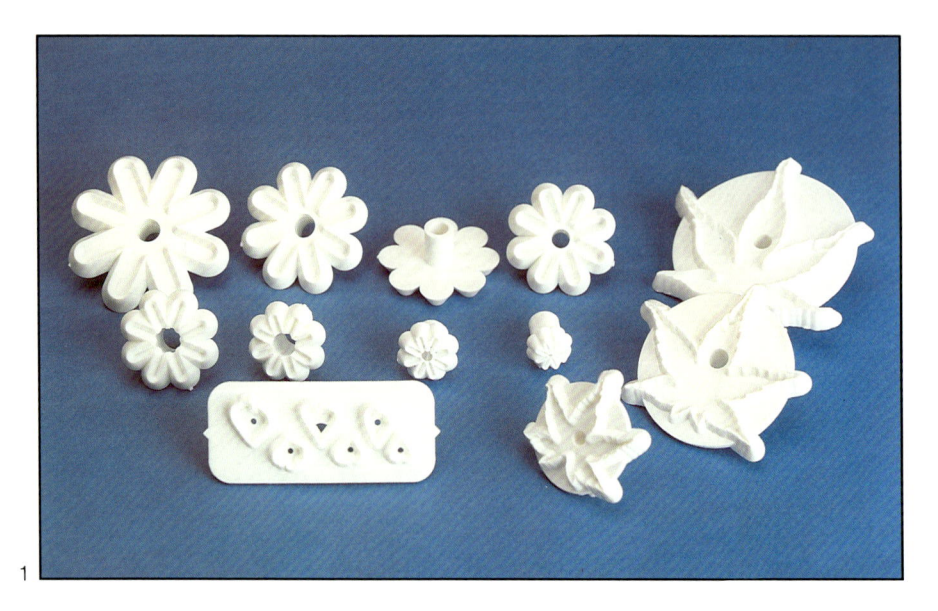
1

THE NEW CUTTERS *(See Illustration 1).*
(Full size shapes are shown in Illustrations 2 & 3).
1. The Daisy Cutters (DY1, DY2, DY3, DY4, DY5, DY6, DY7, DY8). This
range of eight petalled flowers is one of the most comprehensive from the
size point of view – the DY8 must be the smallest currently available at
10mm. The rounded ends suit many different types of flower, while, with a
quick flick of the balling tool (OP1) or veining tool (OP2) they can be made
pointed, if required.
2. The Japanese Maple Leaf Cutters (JM1, JM2, JM3). These delicate
shapes have been faithfully copied from the natural leaves, specially
collected in Japan! They can provide a beautiful setting for many types of
sugar flower, and can make a very dramatic Bonsai tree when used alone.
3. Maidenhair Fern Leaf Cutter (MF1). This cutter cuts out 6 different
leaves at each press, which is about as many as you can process before
the paste dries out. It has a unique feature which enables you to leave a
thickened portion on **each** leaf, for wiring, at the first cut.

THE NEW TOOLS *(See Illustrations 4, 5 & 5A).*
4. The Orchard Pad (PD1). This innovative design is a uniquely textured
foam pad for balling or softening petals or leaves more conveniently and
quicker, instead of using your hand. It is non-stick and therefore does not
need to be covered in cornflour; it does not get hot; thus it does not dry out
your paste so quickly. You can ball right round the petal in one continuous
movement, which is a great help on the new multi-petal flowers.
It is firmer than the sponge normally used for cupping and is washable.
The standard pad is white, which meets the EEC requirements for food
contact materials. We also have a black version which is ideal for
demonstrators.

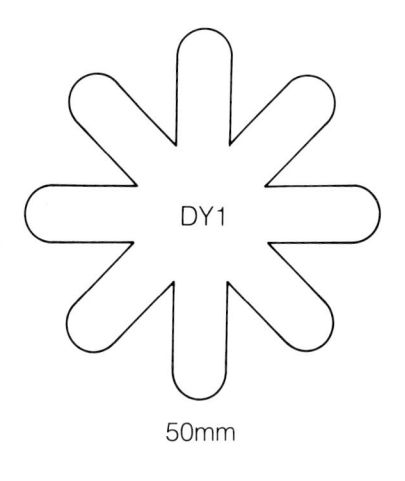

DY1

50mm

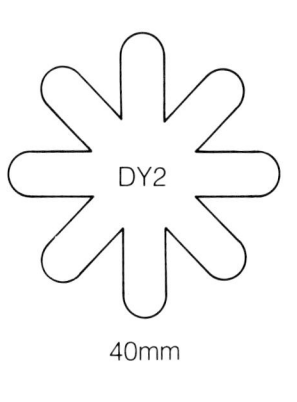

DY2

40mm

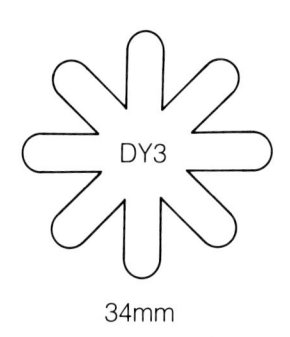

DY3

34mm

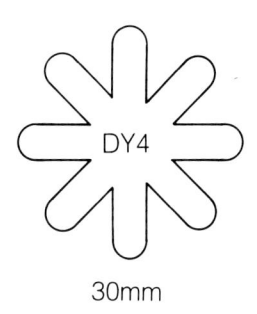

DY4

30mm

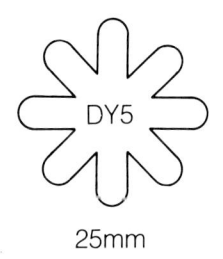

DY5

25mm

DY6

20mm

DY7
15mm

DY8
10mm

2

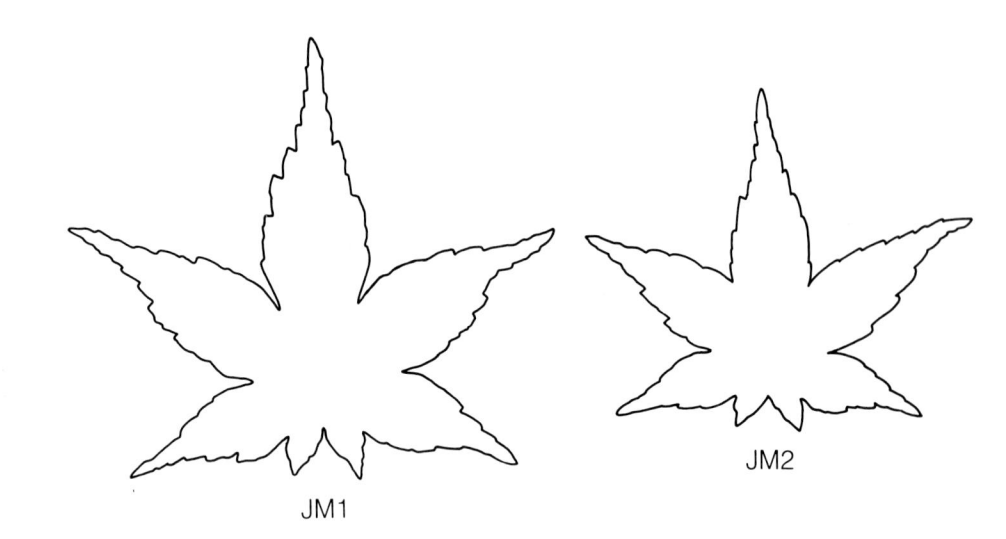

JM1

JM2

JM3

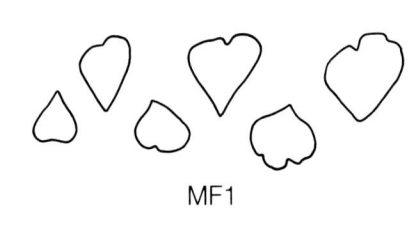

MF1

EGF5 + EGF8

4

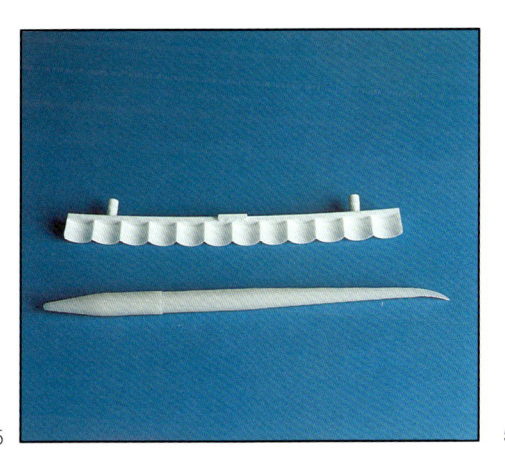

5

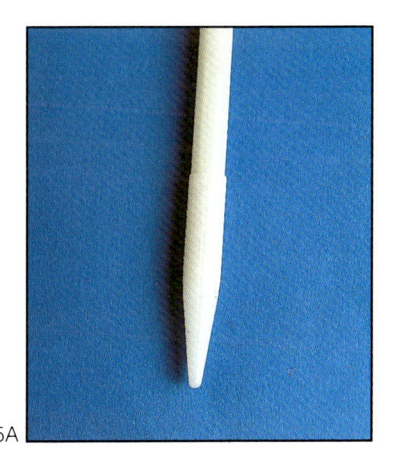

5A

5. Petal Veining Tool (OP2). This unique tool is double-ended, with one tapered finely fluted end (See Illustration 5A) for veining **petals**, either separately, or when assembled into a flower, and the other end has a single veining marker for veining leaves or similar.

To use – roll the finely fluted end lightly across the soft petal supporting it on the back by placing your finger behind it or by leaving it on the pad. The pointed shape means that you can vein petals that have already been assembled into a flower, provided they are still soft. On larger petals roll **again** with the tool at a slight angle to the previous indentations. This gives a very natural looking crisscross effect.

6. Additional Fluted Blade for the Endless Garrett Frill Cutter (FGF8). This repeats the pattern of the fixed blade on the body of the Endless Cutter (EGF5) see Book 5, and can therefore be used to make strips of material of any length, in three widths, with identical fluting on each side, for Broderie Anglaise, embossing or similar decorative work.

This single Endless Garrett Frill cutter set (EGF5, EGF6, EGF7, EGF8) can now therefore produce 15 different frill shapes of any length for your cake borders.

How to make Applique *(See Illustration 6).*
This technique enables you to build up a picture with a 3D effect, very easily. Two typical pictures are described to illustrate the various techniques which can be used.
I use the Orchard series of Five-petal cutters F5 to F10 as described in Book 5, and the Orchard series of Blossom cutters F2L, F2, F2M and F2S as described in Book 2.
Picture A.
1. Roll out white pastillage about 1/8" (4mm) thick and cut out 1 – oval plaque (P4 or P5). Leave overnight to dry.
2. Paint a stalk on the plaque.
3. Roll out Green paste, cut out and vein 4 – rose leaves (R7 leaf & R10 veiner)- see Book 1. Attach to the plaque with a little Royal Icing.
4. Roll out Pink paste and cut out 11 – small blossoms using F2S. Turn over the paste and press out blossoms with the balling tool (OP1) (See Illustration 23). This gives a much better edge to the blossoms. Repeat for 5 – Yellow blossoms using F2S. Attach to plaque with Royal Icing by the following simple method:–
Pipe a spot of Royal Icing on the plaque, then place the piping tube into the centre of a blossom, press out a tiny amount of icing and lift the blossom onto the spot of Royal Icing on the plaque. Release the pressure and repeat for the remaining blossoms.
5. Pipe stalks and leaves with Green Royal Icing, using a Beckenal '0' or '00' piping tube.
6. Roll out Pink paste and cut out 1 – Five-petalled flower (F5). Place on the pad (PD1), soften the edges with the balling tool (OP1) and stick to the plaque with Royal Icing.
7. Repeat Step 6 for 1 – Pink F7, but then stick to the centre of the F5 with rose water, alternating the petals.
8. Roll out Yellow paste and cut out 1 – larger blossom using F2L. Place on sponge and cup the centre with the balling tool. Stick in the centre of F7 with rose water. Pipe a bulb of White Royal Icing in the centre of the F2L blossom.
9. Roll out Pink and Mauve flowerpaste and cut out 3 – butterflies (See Template 7). Fold down the centre and stick to the plaque with Royal Icing.
TEMPLATES. To use a template, make a paper copy by tracing or photocopying and cut round the outline. Place pattern on paste and cut round.

Picture B. *(See Illustration 8).*

1. Roll out White pastillage about 1/8" (4mm) thick and cut out 1 – oval fluted plaque (P5). Leave to dry overnight.
2. Paint green stalk on plaque.
3. Roll out 4 – elongated sausages of Green paste, flatten, mark centre vein with the veining tool (OP2) and stick to the plaque with Royal Icing.
4. Roll out White paste and cut out 5 – Five-petalled flowers (F8). Form the flowers (see Diagram 9 and Illustration 10)). Fold Petal 5 over 4, 3 over 5, 1 over 3 and 2 over 1. Tuck in to form a triangular shape. Attach to the plaque with Royal Icing.
5. Repeat Step 4 with 3 – Pale Pink F8.
6. Repeat Step 4 with 3 – Dark Pink F8.
7. Roll out Pale Pink paste and cut out 1 – bow, 2 – bow tails and 1 – small strip, with the straight blade (EGF6). Frill the ends of the bow with a frilling tool (FT1) (See Illustration 10).
8. Stick the tails to the plaque with Royal Icing and then the bow on top. Moisten the strip with rose water and wrap round the centre of the bow.
9. Roll out Mauve paste and cut out 1 – butterfly (B1) (See Template 7). Fold in the centre, dust the edges Pink with a soft brush and attach to the plaque with Royal Icing.
10. Roll out Pale Pink paste and cut out 12 – F2S blossoms. (Turn the paste over). Attach to the plaque with Royal Icing as before.

7

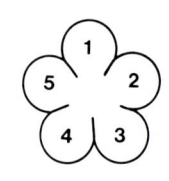

9

10

8

11

12

How to make the Decorative Frills *(See Illustration 11)*.

These frills use the additional blade (EGF8) for the Endless Garrett Frill Cutter Set (EGF5, EGF6, EGF7) previously described in Book 5.

1. Remove the existing detachable blades from the body (EGF5) and insert the new blade (EGF8) into any of the three sets of holes – Wide, Medium or Narrow.

2. Roll out sugarpaste to a suitable length and press the cutter into the paste. Lift off, move along, line up the cutter with the previous cuts and press down. Repeat as required until the desired length of frill has been reached. Remove the surplus material.

3. Frill one or both edges by holding a frilling tool (FT1) flat on the board and rolling firmly back and forward, moving along and repeating the movement as often as required.

4. A decorative feature can now be placed in the centre of the frill, by embossing with a suitable tool, button or cutter, such as the holly leaf cutters (H1-4), or the blossom cutter (F2S) and then pop a little petal dust on each blossom. Alternatively Broderie Anglaise may be used as follows:–(See Illustration 11 and Template 12).
1. Prepare a pattern by photocopying a suitable design from your embroidery books and then open out the holes in the paper with a sharp hat pin. Cut off the torn paper from the back with scissors and then place the pattern in the desired position on the paste while it is still soft.
2. Push through the holes with a cocktail stick, rocking it slightly for the larger holes, then move the pattern and repeat as required.
Stick the frill to the cake with a little water while still soft.
3. When dry, pipe **round** the holes in the paste with Royal Icing using a '0' or '00' piping tube. Petal dust the base of the frill.
NB: The pattern can be kept for future use.

13

How to make the Forget-me-not *(See Illustration 13).*
1. Roll out Blue flowerpaste and cut out blossoms with the F2 or F2M cutters (See Book 2). Turn the paste over onto a sponge and push out the blossoms with a balling tool. This gives a better finished edge. Place on a board.
2. Cut between the petals with the straight blade (EGF6), remove to the pad (PD1) and press a small balling tool or glass-headed pin (See Illustration 23) just inside each petal to cup them slightly. Turn over, press in the centre with the glass-headed pin and place into a flower stand. (See Illustration 14).
3. Glue the top of a Yellow stamen and push through the centre of the blossom. Leave to dry.

14

15

How to make the Celendine *(See Illustration 15)*.
1. Tape 6 Yellow stamens onto the end of a 33 gauge wire with florists tape.
2. Roll out Bright Lemon paste and cut out 1 – DY6 daisy. Place on the pad (PD1) and stroke each petal out with the veining tool (OP2) to form a point. Mark a centre vein down each petal (See Illustration 16). Place in a flower stand.
3. Glue the base of the stamens and thread through the centre of the petal. Leave to dry.

16

17

18

How to make the Linium *(See Illustration 17)*.

1. Tape 5- Yellow stamens onto the end of a 26 gauge wire with florists tape.

2. Roll out White flowerpaste and cut out 1 – F7. Soften the edges with the balling tool (OP1) on the Orchard Pad (PD1) and roll the petal veining tool (OP2) over the petals. Place on a sponge and press in the centre (See Illustration 18).

3. Glue the base of the stamens and thread the wire through the centre of the petal. Place in flower stand to dry.

4. Calyx. Roll out Green paste and cut out 1 – R15. Soften the edges on the pad, glue the centre and thread onto the wire up to the base of the flower. When dry, dust the centre yellow and the sides bluey-violet.

How to make the Apple Blossom *(See Illustration 19).*
1. Tape about 13 or 14 – Yellow stamens to the end of a piece of 26 gauge wire with florists tape.
2. Roll out White flowerpaste and cut out 1 – five-petal flower (F8,F9 or F10). Place on the pad (PD1),and soften the edges with the balling tool (OP1). Place each petal in turn over your finger and roll the petal veining tool (OP2) over the petals.
3. Place on a sponge and circle round the centre with the balling tool to cup it or place over a suitably sized hole on the Flower Stand (S1) and press in the centre to cup it (See Illustration 20.).
4. Moisten the stamens with a little glue, place the flower in a flower stand and thread the wire through the petal until the stamens rest in the flower. Leave 24 hours to dry.
5. The Calyx. Roll out Green flowerpaste and cut out one calyx (R15). Soften the edges, glue the base of the flower and thread the calyx onto the wire, pressing onto the underside of the flower.
6. Glue the base of the calyx, thread a small ball of Green paste onto the wire for the pip and press round the base of the calyx.
7. Dust the petals Rose Pink and the centre of the flower Green.
8. Apple Bud. Hook and glue the end of a 28 gauge wire, push into a small ball of White flowerpaste. Dry overnight.
9. Roll out White flowerpaste and cut out one five-petal flower (F9). Soften the edges with the balling tool and mark with the petal veining tool (OP2). Turn the petal over.
10. Cup into the centre, glue the flowerpaste on the wire and thread through the petal. The veining should be on the outside.
11. Glue one petal over the top of the ball and the remaining four petals interleave round the bud.
12. The Calyx. Roll out Green flowerpaste and cut out one calyx (R15). Soften the edges, glue the base of the bud and thread the calyx onto the wire, wrapping round the bud.
13. Glue the base of the calyx, thread a small ball of Green paste onto the wire for the pip and press round the base of the calyx.
14. Leaves. Roll out Green paste and cut out 5 or 6 – leaves for each branch using the Template 21. Mark veins with the veining tool (OP2).
15. To make the stem. Fold 4 strands of 22 gauge wire in half and then in half again giving a bundle of 16 wires and then tape them together with brown florists tape. Run the back of a pair of scissors along the stem to merge the tape and wires.
16. Tape the buds and flowers in groups of 3 or 4 down the stem, with about 3 leaves under each set of flowers.

19

20

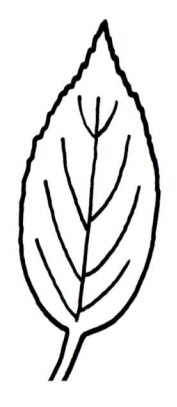

21

22

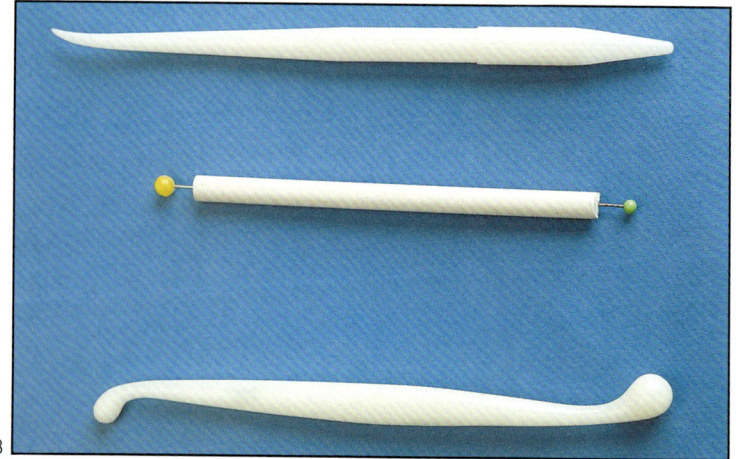

23

How to make the Small Daisy *(See Illustration 15).*
1. Calyx. Glue the end of a 33 gauge green wire with rose water and push into a small ball of Green paste. Roll between finger and thumb to form a sausage shape and pull the sausage up until it just overhangs the end of the wire. Indent the top of the sausage with the small end of the balling tool (OP1) to make a cup for the flower to sit in.
(See Illustration 22).
2. Roll out White paste thinly (a little thicker for DY8) – leave a thicker portion at one edge so that you can pick up the paste easily – and press in a small daisy cutter DY6, 7 or 8 (because they are so small they only have the number marked on the back), lift the cutter up and repeat several times. Carefully move all the paste onto a sponge and press out the flowers with a balling tool (OP1 or smaller tools, such as a glass headed pin pushed into a piece of dowelling – See Illustration 23).
3. If desired to make them look even daintier, move a flower onto the board and cut each petal in half lengthways (do not use a sharp metal blade since it may damage the board). The straight plastic blade from the Endless Garrett Frill set (EGF6) is a useful tool for this purpose.
4. Place onto the pad (PD1), soften petals with the balling tool (OP1) and cup the centre. Flick over, moisten the centre of the calyx with rose water and push onto the centre of the back of the flower. Turn over and press in the centre of the flower so that it sticks properly.
5. Press a small ball of yellow sugarpaste onto a piece of tulle (Bride's net). Moisten the centre of the daisy, turn the tulle over, place your finger on the centre and press the marked paste into the centre of the daisy – marked side uppermost. Remove the tulle and leave to dry.
6. When dry, dust the outer edge of the petals pale pink with a soft brush.

24

How to make the Jiffy Flower *(See Illustration 24)*.

These fantasy flowers are so named because they can be made 'in a jiffy!'. They can be made in any size or colour to complement your sprays or bouquets.

1. Hook the end of a 24 gauge wire. Make a 'Mexican Hat' from a small sausage of paste pressed into one of the holes in the 'Mexican Hat' Adaptor (M1) – (see Book 7). Stand the 'hat' on the board and roll out from the centre to the edge with the plain Frilling tool (FT1) to thin out the paste. Make sure the crown of the hat is thin enough for the cutter to fit over.§

2. Place the cutter F8 over the stem and cut out one flower. Dip the hook in rose water and thread wire through the centre of the flower. Roll the back of the flower between your fingers to elongate it. Place on the pad and frill the edges by pressing firmly around the edge of the petals with the balling tool (OP1). (See Illustration 25).

3. Roll out flowerpaste and cut out 1 – F8 flat. Glue the centre of the lst flower and place the flat flower on top, interleaving the petals. Then make a hole in the centre with the sharp end of the veining tool (OP2), cut a bunch of stamens and press into the centre. Prop with cloud drift* and leave to dry in a flower stand. (See Illustration 26). When dry, petal dust with a soft brush according to your colour scheme.

§ With the very smallest cutters the centre hole is not big enough for this method. In this case hold the cutter upside down and press the head of the golf tee onto the cutter with your fingers. (See Illustration 27). Alternatively using the Mexican Hat Adaptor, leave the paste in the adaptor and thin out with a rolling pin. Make a small mark with a pin in the centre and then cut out the petal, using the mark to centre the cutter.
* 'Cloud drift' is Acrylic fibre material teased out, as used in duvots. It has the advantage over cotton wool that it does not stick.

28   29

How to make the Maidenhair Fern *(See Illustration 28)*.

There are two methods a) & b). Use whichever suits you best. In either case first colour some White 'Scientific wire' (very fine, approx. 36 gauge) brown by putting some liquid brown colour onto a piece of sponge, laying the wire on top, press the sponge together and pull the wire through. This is a quick way of colouring the wire.

Method a) 1. Roll out Green flowerpaste, slightly thicker than usual, and cut out the leaves with the Maidenhair Fern cutter (MF1).

2. Take one of the leaves and pop it onto your finger with the edge hanging well down. Roll the petal veining tool (OP2) over 3/4 of the leaf area to thin it and vein it, leaving a thick edge for wiring.

3. Glue the end of a 36 gauge wire and, holding the thick edge of the leaf between finger and thumb, push in the wire. Soften the outside edge of the leaf with a balling tool to give it a more natural look. Leave to dry. Dust the edges brown to highlight the leaves.

Method b) 4. Roll out Green flowerpaste thinly but form a narrow ridge in the centre. Line up the two pointers on the ends of the Maidenhair Fern cutter (MF1) with the ridge and press down. Lift up, peel away the surplus material and each of the 6 leaves will already have a thickened portion for wiring.

5. Proceed as for Steps 2 and 3 above.

6. To assemble (See Illustration 29). Tape a set of leaves (6) together one behind the other in an ascending order. Bend each leaf out sideways to form a fan shape. Tape 3 sets together, one in the centre and one each side. This forms a spray which can be used as a setting for many types of flower.

30

How to make the Lilac – *syringa vulgaris* *(Sec Illustration 30).*

1. Calyx. Dip the end of a 33 gauge wire into rose water and push into a small ball of Lilac paste. Roll between finger and thumb to form a sausage shape and pull the sausage up till it just overhangs the end of the wire. Indent the top of the sausage with the small end of the balling tool (OP1) to make a cup for the flower to sit in (See Illustration 31).

2. Roll out lilac coloured flowerpaste and cut out one daphne (D1). Cut off the tips of the daphne and place on the pad (PD1). Ball around the inside edge of each petal with a small balling tool or glass-headed pin to curl over.

31

32

3. Place on sponge and press in centre to cup. Flick over, moisten the centre of the calyx with rose water and push onto the centre of the back of the flower. Turn over and press in the centre of the flower so that it sicks properly.

4. Press a tiny indentation into the centre with the single end of the veining tool (OP2).

5. Repeat Steps 2 to 4 until you have about 60 flowers for each lilac panticle.

6. Assembly. (See Illustrations 32 & 33). Tape the flowers together in two's and three's with green florists tape. Wrap the tape a couple of times about 1/4" **below** the base of the flower and then, holding the tape, pull down the wire so that the flower just touches the top of the tape. Cut off the surplus wires at an angle to avoid a lumpy stem. When dry, dust the centre a darker shade of lilac.

7. Leaves. Roll out Green paste and, leaving a thick edge for wiring, cut out a leaf using Template 34A. Mark veins with the veining tool (OP2). Glue the end of a 30 gauge wire and, holding between finger and thumb, push the wire into the thickened end of the leaf. Ball the edges to thin them out then leave to dry. Petal dust a darker green to give a more natural look. 'Steam' the leaves to give a sheen (Book 5) (See Illustration 34). To assemble tape onto a 24 gauge wire.

33

34

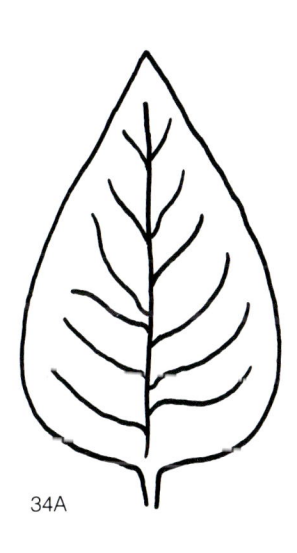

34A

35

36

How to make the Flowering Cherry – *Okame (Japanese Cherry Tree)* *(See Illustration 35).*

1. Tape together about 10 yellow stamens onto the end of a 24 gauge wire.
2. Colour the flowerpaste with Claret, Mulberry and Grape Violet paste colours. Roll out and cut out one five-petal flower (F7 or F8).
3. Soften the edges with the balling tool (OP1), then, supporting each petal with your finger, roll the petal veining tool (OP2) over each petal in turn. Place in the Flower Stand (S1) and cup in the centre of the flower with the balling tool. (See Illustration 36).
4. Put a little glue on the base of the stamens and thread the wire through the centre of the flower, pressing the stamens gently against the petals. Leave to dry on the flower stand. Spread out the stamens.
5. Calyx. Roll out Brown or very Dark Maroon paste and cut out one calyx (R15). Glue base of flower and thread on calyx.
6. Buds. Make an hook in the end of a 33 gauge brown wire. Glue a small ball of the brown paste round the hook. Leave to dry.
7. Repeat Steps 2 and 3.
8. Put a little glue on the ball. Thread the wire through the centre of the flower and cup around the ball.
9. Repeat Step 5.
10. Leaves. Roll out a sausage of Green flowerpaste, taper at one end -the base, flatten out and mark the veins with the veining tool (OP2). Thin out the outside edge with the balling tool (OP1) and glue the end of a 30 gauge wire and insert into the base.
11. To make the stem, fold 4 strands of 22 gauge wire in half and then in half again giving a bundle of 16 wires and tape them together with brown florists tape.
12. Tape the flowers and leaves onto the central stem leaving a couple of inches of the stem protruding beyond the topmost flower.
13. Tape the buds and flowers to the stem with brown florists tape in groups of 5, with the leaves at the base.

37

38

How to make Chrysanthemums with the Daisy Cutters.

How to make the Small Chrysanthemum *(See Illustration 37)*.

1. Make a small hook in the end of a 24 gauge wire, dip into rose water and pop a small ball of yellow paste on top.

2. Roll out pink coloured flowerpaste and cut out two DY7 daisies. Cover remaining paste. Place on the Orchard Pad (PD1) and ball from the end of the petals into the centre to curl them.

3. Moisten the centre of one and place the other on top, interleaving the petals. Put a small amount of rose water onto the centre, thread the wire through the centre and cup round the yellow centre. (See Illustration 38).

4. Cut out three DY6, and repeat Steps 2 and 3.

5. Cut out two DY5, and repeat Steps 2 and 3.

6. Leave to dry on something like a cotton reel so that the lower petals gently bend back (See Illustration 41).

39

How to make the White Chrysanthemum *(See Illustration 39).*

1. Make a small hook in the end of a 24 gauge wire, dip into rose water and push into a small ball of White flowerpaste.

2. Roll out white flowerpaste and cut out two DY7 daisies. Cover remaining paste. Put the flowers on the pad (PD1) and stroke out each petal from the tip to the base with a small glass-headed pin, so that they curl up. Repeat inside each petal to curl over.

3. Pop onto sponge and press in the centre with the balling tool (OP1). Apply rose water to the centre of one petal and place the other on top, interleaving the petals. (N.B: The single tip of the petal veining tool (OP2) is very useful for arranging the interleaving of the petals).

4. Apply rose water to the ball, thread the two petals onto the wire and stroke the petals around the ball with your fingertips. (See Illustration 40).

5. Repeat Steps 2 and 3 for two DY6 – the next largest daisy cutter. Apply 'glue' to the centre of the top petal and thread onto the wire, interleaving the petals with the first layer. Press the top of the petals **gently** inwards with your fingertips. Place in a flower stand.

6. Repeat Step 5 five more times for daisy cutters DY5, DY4, DY3, DY2, and DY1. Use the small end of the balling tool (OP1) for DY5.

7. Repeat Steps 2 & 3 for two more DY1, **then turn the petals over**, place on sponge, press the balling tool in the centre, apply glue to the centre and sides of the petals, and thread onto the wire as before. Leave to dry on a cotton reel or similar so that the lower petals can bend down. (See Illustration 41). When dry tape to thicker wire, say 20 gauge.

40

41

42

43   44

How to make the Cerise Chrysanthemum (See Illustration 42).

1. Hook the end of a 24 gauge wire, dip into rose water and push into a small ball of Pale Green paste.

2. Colour some flowerpaste with Claret, Mulberry and Grape Violet paste colours, as for the Flowering Cherry. Roll out the paste a little thicker than normal and cut out 2 – DY8 daisies. Cut each petal down the centre with the straight blade (EGF6) and part them.

3. Put them on the pad (PD1) and gently press each petal with a balling tool to slightly widen and soften it. Pop on sponge and press in the centre to cup them slightly.

4. Glue the centre of the petals and place one on top of the other, interleaving the petals. Thread onto the wire and wrap them round the green ball. (See Illustration 43).

5. Repeat Steps 2, 3 and 4 for 2 – DY7 and DY6.

6. Repeat Steps 2 and 3 for 2 – DY5 and 2- DY4 but do **not** cut down the centres. Press out the ends with a small balling tool or glass-headed pin so that they become pointed. Vein by rolling the petal veining tool (OP2) over them. Apply glue to the centre of the petals and place one on top of the other, interleaving the petals. (See Illustration 44).

Pop on sponge and press in the centre to cup. Thread onto the wire and press up to the previous petals.

7. Repeat Step 6 for 2 – DY3, 2 – DY2 and 2 – DY1. Put the assembled flower on a cotton reel so that the lower petals can bend down a little more.

8. Calyx. Roll out Green paste and cut out 1- DY6. Soften the edges, glue the centre and thread onto the wire up to the petals. Leave to dry.

9. When dry, dust in a darker colour in the centre of the flower and then tape it onto a thicker wire.

45

46

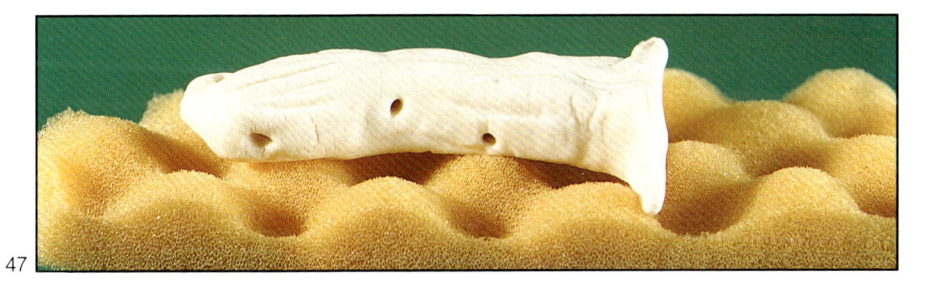

47

How to make the Bonsai Tree *(See Illustration 45).*

1. Make, say four branches first by folding 4 strands of 22 gauge wire in half and then in half again giving a bundle of 16 wires, and then taping them together with brown florists tape. Set to the desired shapes.

2. Form the trunk from pastillage by modelling with your fingers, first making a sausage shape and parting the bottom to form a spread out base. (See Illustration 46). Then stroke in the bark contours with the veining tool (OP2). Push the ends of the branches into the required positions and remove. Leave to dry on sponge (See Illustration 47). Extra holes **can** be made later with a bradawl if absolutely necessary. Add to the bark effect by moistening different shades of sugarpaste and pressing and stroking onto the trunk to build it up (See Illustration 50).

3. When dry, colour with brown, green and red petal dust to suit.

4. Colour some 30 gauge wire Red for the leaves, by putting some red liquid colour onto a piece of sponge, laying the white wire on top, press sponge together and pull the wire through.

5. Roll out Yellow, Green and/or Red flowerpaste, leaving a thickened edge and cut out about 20 Japanese Maple Leaves (JM1, JM2 & JM3), positioning the base of the cutter over the thickened edge of the paste. Take care when peeling off the surplus material since the fronds are very delicate.

Ball each frond down towards the bottom centre so that the paste is still thicker there. Hold the Red 30 gauge wire (from Step 4) between finger and thumb, dip the end in rose water and insert into the base of the leaf. Vein by stroking one vein down the centre of each frond with the single end of the veining tool (OP2) to obtain a natural look. Soften the edges with the balling tool.

6. Add additional colouring by dusting with Red, Purple or Green petal dust. When dry, steam each leaf for a few seconds (See Book 5).

48

49

50

7. Tape onto the branches with brown florists tape as required. Then fix the branches into the holes in the trunk with Royal Icing. When dry, dust with a mixture of Brown/Green & Black. (See Illustration 48).

8. The Stand. (See Illustration 49). Roll out thick sugarpaste and cut out an oval shape, about 4" long. Indent round the edge, about 1/8" in, with the veining tool (OP2), and, while still soft, press in the base of the trunk of the bonsai tree and remove, to form a locating socket. Make four small balls of paste and flatten to form feet for underneath the stand. Glue on when dry. Fix the trunk in position with a little Royal Icing.

9. To make the 'earth'. Crush up some old dried sugarpaste in a plastic bag. Then prepare a mixture of Brown, Black and Green petal dust and shake the bag to mix it into the crushed sugarpaste until it is an even colour. Before placing the earth onto the stand, brush the face of the stand with brown petal dust, so that should there be any gaps in the earth they will not show (See Illustration 50).

51

How to make the Wedding Tops *(See Illustration 51)*.
(Ideas contributed by Shirley Cook).
These tops are self supporting and can be easily removed from the cake.
The Heart Shaped Spray
1. First make a suitable selection of flowers and leaves. Suggested quantities and wire sizes[ ] as follows:–
Blossoms for the Heart Shape:10- large (F2L), 8- medium (F2), 12- small (F2S).
Peach rose: 1- bud[26/28g], 4- open roses[26g].
White blossoms [24g]: 4 sets each comprising 1 bud, 1 small (F2S), and 1 medium (F2) all taped together, and all dusted peach in the centre.
Rose leaves[26g]: 2- small (R7), 4 medium (R6) – {Veiners (R10) and (R9)}.
Baby's breath: 10 sprays[30g].
Pale Blue ribbons: 3- Thread ribbons, 6- double loop ribbons.

52

2. To make the ribbons:–
Thread Ribbon (See Illustration 52). Tear 2" wide florists paper ribbon (Pale Blue) down the centre into two halves. Place a 7" length in the Ribbon Shredder with 1" projecting (to hold). Then press down the top of the shredder firmly and pull the ribbon through evenly for about 5" (See Illustration 53). This will leave the ribbon with two uncut ends. Fold in half lengthways and cut ends evenly. Pinch ends together and tape to 26 gauge wire.
Double Ribbon Loops (See Illustration 54). Fold the end of about 1/4" wide ribbon (Pale Blue) away from you to make 1 loop, then come up the back and fold back again slightly higher up to make the second loop. Come back up once more to form a tail and cut off. Curl the tail by pulling it over the back of a pair of scissors (See Illustration 55). Split the tail in two lengthways. Pinch firmly together at the bottom of the loops and cut off the remaining ribbon. Bend a 26 gauge wire in half and place the bend over the pinched end of the ribbon (See Illustration 56). Twist as tightly as possible and wind one leg of the wire round the ribbon and the other leg of the wire. Twist several times to trap the ribbon. Cut wires to the required length (3"). Tape the wires to neaten. Pull the loops into shape.

3. * Make the heart shape first (row 4) so that the blossoms can dry.
The flowers are taped together with White or Green florists tape in groups or rows, and each row is taped slightly below the previous row.
Row 1; 1 Peach rose bud, 3 Blue thread ribbons. (See Illustration 52).

53

54

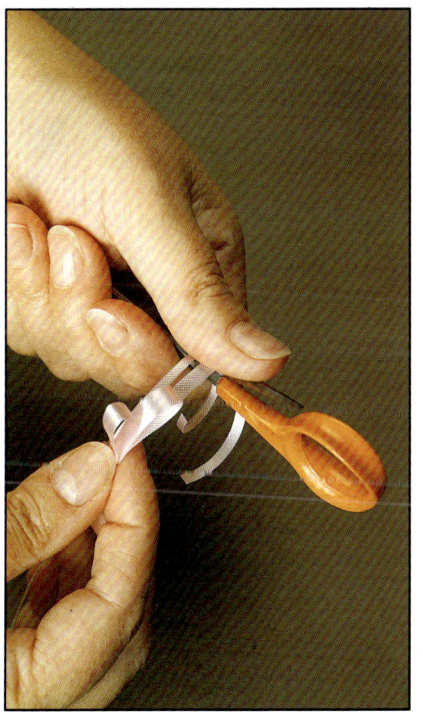

55

56

57

58   59

Row 2; 4 Peach open roses, 4 sets White blossoms, 4 baby's breath sprays (See Illustration 57).

Row 3; 4 medium rose leaves, 2 small rose leaves. (See Illustration 58)

Row 4; Heart Shape*. Bend the top of two 14" lengths of 24 gauge wire into a hook. Thread 5 large blossoms, 4 medium and 6 small onto the top 7" of each wire, each fixed with a dot of Royal Icing. (See Illustration 58). Bend the top 7" of each wire into a half heart shape. Hook the two top ends together. Tape the previous rows onto the straight parts of the 24 gauge wire just below the heart shape.

Row 5; 6 double loop ribbons, 6 baby's breath sprays.

4. To form the legs, turn the spray over and divide the remaining stem into 4 parts. Bend outwards to form 4 legs and tape each leg separately (See Illustration 59). Cut to length. The end of each leg should be just inside the tip of the last rose leaf. Turn upright, place two fingers underneath-scissor shape- while pressing the stem down onto the table to adjust the angle of the feet.

60

The Pyramid *(See Illustration 60).*

1. First make a suitable selection of flowers and leaves. Suggested quantities as follows:–

White Daphne: 12- buds, 13- small (D2), 11- medium (D1) [33g].
Mauve Daphne: 13- buds, 12- small (D2), 12- medium (D1) [33g].
White Daisy: 8- small (DY8), 7- medium (DY7) [33g].
White Jiffy Flower: 8- small (F9) [28g] §
Pink chrysanthemums: 6- 1"dia. (DY3 – DY8) [26g]. Size of a 10P piece.
Maidenhair Fern (MF1): 8- sprays [36g] (1 spray = 4 leaves)
                       6- sets (1 set = 3 sprays)

(§ The Jiffy flowers can be edged with pink and given a pink centre, or similarly with mauve.)

2. The individual flowers are taped up onto a thicker wire [24g] about 7 or 8" long with white or green florist's tape. The spray and sets are taped to a single wire [24g]. These are then taped in groups or rows.

Each row is spread out a little further and taped below the previous one. [1 set = 1 bud + 1 small & 1 medium flower taped together onto 26g].

1st or Top row; 1 stem of 24 gauge wire (8/9" long), 1 mauve bud, 1 small White Daphne, 2 medium White Daphne.

2nd row; 2 medium Daisies, 2 Jiffy flowers, 2 sprays of Maidenhair Fern. (See Illustration 61).

61 62

3rd row; 1 set Mauve Daphne (3), 1 set White Daphne (3), 1 Jiffy flower, 1 Maidenhair Fern spray. Repeat twice more. (See Illustration 62).
4th row; [Branching unit: 1 bud, 1 small Daphne, 1 small Daisy, 1 Jiffy flower, all taped together], 1 set Mauve Daphne (3), 1 Chrysanthemum. Repeat twice more. Insert a spray of Maidenhair Fern behind the Chrysanthemums. (See Illustration 63)
5th row; 1 Chrysanthemum, 1 set Mauve Daphne (3), 1 set White Daphne (3), shredded ribbon. Repeat twice more.
Base row; 1 set Maidenhair Fern (3), 1 set Mauve Daphne (3), 1 set White Daphne (3), a branching unit of 2 small Daisies and 1 medium. Repeat twice more. Insert a set of Maidenhair Fern underneath the Daphnes and Daisies 3 times to complete.
3. The flowers should have taken up about 5 inches of the stem, so, to form the legs, turn the spray over and divide the remaining stem into 3 parts. Bend outwards to form a tripod and tape each leg separately (See Illustration 64). Cut to length. The end of each leg should be just inside the maidenhair fern. Turn upright, place two fingers underneath – scissor shape- while pressing the stem down onto the table to adjust the angle of the feet.

63

64

RECIPES

Flowerpaste A. 250g ($^1/_2$lb) Bakels 'Pettinice' or Craigmillars'Pastello'only.
1 teaspoon (5ml) Gum Tragacanth.
Rub 'Trex' on your hands and knead ingredients together until elastic. Wrap tightly in plastic and store in an airtight container. Leave for 24 hours. There is no need to refrigerate. This paste keeps well if worked through say, once a week. Always keep tightly wrapped.

Flowerpaste D. 450g sieved icing sugar
5mls Gum Tragacanth and 20mls Carboxymethylcellulose (CMC)
10mls powdered Gelatine soaked in 25mls cold water
10mls white fat (Trex or Spry, not lard)
10mls liquid Glucose
45mls egg white

Sieve all the icing sugar into a greased* (Trex) mixing bowl. Add the gums to the sugar. Warm the mixture in a microwave oven 3 x 50 secs on medium setting, stirring in between.
Sprinkle the gelatine over the water in a cup and allow to sponge. Put the cup in hot, not boiling, water until clear. Add the white fat and liquid glucose. Heat the dough hook, add the dissolved ingredients and the egg white to the warmed sugar, and beat on the lowest speed until all the ingredients are combined. At this stage the mixture will be a dingy beige colour. Turn the machine to maximum speed and mix until the mixture becomes white and stringy. Grease your hands and remove the paste from the machine. Pull and stretch the paste several times. Knead together and then cut into 4 sections. Knead each section again and place in a plastic bag, then in an airtight container and keep in the refrigerator. Let it mature for 24 hours.
This paste dries very quickly so, when ready to use, cut off only a very small piece and re-seal the remainder. Work it well with your fingers. It should be the consistency of well chewed chewing gum. If it should be a little too hard and crumbly, add a little egg white and white fat. The fat slows down the drying process and the egg white makes it more pliable.
Keep coloured paste in a separate container.

* This eases the strain on the machine considerably.

Pastillage. 500g icing sugar
10g Gelatine
30g Royal Icing
30g cornflour
60g water

Sprinkle the gelatine over the water in a cup and allow to sponge. Put the cup in hot, not boiling, water until clear. Sift the icing sugar and cornflour into a bowl. Pour the warm gelatine into the centre stirring with a knife, add the Royal Icing and knead until it forms a paste.
Wrap in clingfilm and pop into an airtight container. Leave for a few hours to mature. This paste will keep for several days.

Gum Arabic Glue.
Use proportions of 3:1 of tepid water and Gum Arabic, i.e. 3 teaspoons of water to 1 teaspoon of Gum Arabic. Place in a small glass bottle (8ml) with screw top and brush, or clean nail varnish container and shake well. This saves continually cleaning the brush, and keeps it moist.